LEGIONNAIRES' DISEASE

Anthrax

Avian Flu

Botulism

Campylobacteriosis

Cholera

Ebola

Encephalitis

Escherichia coli Infections

Gonorrhea

Hantavirus Pulmonary Syndrome

Hepatitis

Herpes

HIV/AIDS

Infectious Fungi

Influenza

Legionnaires' Disease

Leprosy

Lyme Disease

Mad Cow Disease (Bovine Spongiform Encephalopathy)

Malaria

Meningitis

Mononucleosis

Pelvic Inflammatory Disease

Plague

Polio

Salmonella

SARS

Smallpox

Streptococcus (Group A)

Staphylococcus aureus Infections

Syphilis

Toxic Shock Syndrome

Tuberculosis

Tularemia

Typhoid Fever

West Nile Virus

DEADLY DISEASES AND EPIDEMICS

LEGIONNAIRES' DISEASE

Jon Zonderman
and
Laurel Shader, M.D.

FOUNDING EDITOR
The Late **I. Edward Alcamo**
Distinguished Teaching Professor of Microbiology,
SUNY Farmingdale

FOREWORD BY
David Heymann
World Health Organization

CHELSEA HOUSE
PUBLISHERS
An imprint of Infobase Publishing

Legionnaires' Disease

Copyright © 2006 by Infobase Publishing

Chelsea House
An imprint of Infobase Publishing
132 West 31st Street
New York NY 10001

Library of Congress Cataloging-in-Publication Data

Zonderman, Jon.
    Legionnaires' disease /Jon Zonderman.
        p. cm.—(Deadly diseases and epidemics)
ISBN 0-7910-8885-5
    1. Legionnaires' disease—Juvenile literature. I. Title. II. Series.
R152.7.Z66 2005
616.2'41—dc22

                                                    2005026622

Chelsea House books are available at special discounts when purchased in bulk quantities for businesses, associations, institutions, or sales promotions. Please call our Special Sales Department in New York at (212) 967-8800 or (800) 322-8755.

You can find Chelsea House on the World Wide Web at http://www.chelseahouse.com

Text design by Terry Mallon
Cover design by Keith Trego

Printed in the United States of America

Bang 21C 10 9 8 7 6 5 4 3 2 1

This book is printed on acid-free paper.

All links and web addresses were checked and verified to be correct at the time of publication. Because of the dynamic nature of the web, some addresses and links may have changed since publication and may no longer be valid.

Table of Contents

Foreword

In the 1960s, many of the infectious diseases that had terrorized generations were tamed. After a century of advances, the leading killers of Americans both young and old were being prevented with new vaccines or cured with new medicines. The risk of death from pneumonia, tuberculosis (TB), meningitis, influenza, whooping cough, and diphtheria declined dramatically. New vaccines lifted the fear that summer would bring polio, and a global campaign was on the verge of eradicating smallpox worldwide. New pesticides like DDT cleared mosquitoes from homes and fields, thus reducing the incidence of malaria, which was present in the southern United States and which remains a leading killer of children worldwide. New technologies produced safe drinking water and removed the risk of cholera and other water-borne diseases. Science seemed unstoppable. Disease seemed destined to all but disappear.

But the euphoria of the 1960s has evaporated.

The microbes fought back. Those causing diseases like TB and malaria evolved resistance to cheap and effective drugs. The mosquito developed the ability to defuse pesticides. New diseases emerged, including AIDS, Legionnaires, and Lyme disease. And diseases which had not been seen in decades re-emerged, as the hantavirus did in the Navajo Nation in 1993. Technology itself actually created new health risks. The global transportation network, for example, meant that diseases like West Nile virus could spread beyond isolated regions and quickly become global threats. Even modern public health protections sometimes failed, as they did in 1993 in Milwaukee, Wisconsin, resulting in 400,000 cases of the digestive system illness cryptosporidiosis. And, more recently, the threat from smallpox, a disease believed to be completely eradicated, has returned along with other potential bioterrorism weapons such as anthrax.

The lesson is that the fight against infectious diseases will never end.

In our constant struggle against disease, we as individuals have a weapon that does not require vaccines or drugs, and that is the warehouse of knowledge. We learn from the history of science that "modern" beliefs can be wrong. In this series of books, for example, you will learn that diseases like syphilis were once thought to be caused by eating potatoes. The invention of the microscope set science on the right path. There are more positive lessons from history. For example, smallpox was eliminated by vaccinating everyone who had come in contact with an infected person. This "ring" approach to smallpox control is still the preferred method for confronting an outbreak, should the disease be intentionally reintroduced.

At the same time, we are constantly adding new drugs, new vaccines, and new information to the warehouse. Recently, the entire human genome was decoded. So too was the genome of the parasite that causes malaria. Perhaps by looking at the microbe and the victim through the lens of genetics we will be able to discover new ways to fight malaria, which remains the leading killer of children in many countries.

Because of advances in our understanding of such diseases as AIDS, entire new classes of anti-retroviral drugs have been developed. But resistance to all these drugs has already been detected, so we know that AIDS drug development must continue.

Education, experimentation, and the discoveries that grow out of them are the best tools to protect health. Opening this book may put you on the path of discovery. I hope so, because new vaccines, new antibiotics, new technologies, and, most importantly, new scientists are needed now more than ever if we are to remain on the winning side of this struggle against microbes.

David Heymann
Executive Director
Communicable Diseases Section
World Health Organization
Geneva, Switzerland

1

A New Disease Is Born

From July 21 to 24, 1976, hundreds of members of the American Legion and their wives gathered in Philadelphia for the 58th annual meetings of the legion and its women's auxiliary. As at previous conventions, members of both groups heard speeches from politicians and from the organizations' leaders. The men held their meetings at one downtown hotel while the women held their meetings at another hotel. Guests stayed at both hotels, and some social events for both groups were held at each hotel. Many attendees came to Philadelphia a day or two early to visit the city's historic attractions.

A couple of days into the proceedings, people who were attending the convention and staying at one of the hotels began to fall ill. They had headaches, fevers, and chills. They felt tired and worn out, and many skipped meeting sessions and sightseeing trips to stay in bed in their hotel rooms. The symptoms were similar to the flu, but the meeting was occurring in the summer; typically, influenza strikes the Northeast states in the late fall and winter.

Many of the legionnaires and their wives developed coughs and became short of breath; some even had chest pains. When these symptoms occurred, these mostly middle-aged and elderly people began showing up in Philadelphia hospitals, where they were diagnosed with pneumonia.

Over the course of a few days, 221 people became ill with this respiratory disease of unknown cause. Although most were attending the American Legion convention, a few of the people who became ill were hotel staff or other hotel guests. Most of those who became ill recovered over time, but 34 people died from their illness.

PNEUMONIA

The term *pneumonia* describes an inflammation of the lungs (Figure 1.1). Pneumonia is not a disease in and of itself. Rather, it is a symptom that is common to any of over 50 different diseases. When pneumonia occurs, it becomes difficult to fully expand the lungs with air, which makes breathing difficult and sometimes very painful.

Pneumonia can be caused by a virus or bacteria, or by **aspiration** (inhaling into the trachea and lungs what is meant for esophagus and the stomach) of items such as food. Bacterial and aspiration pneumonia are treated with antibiotic medications, whereas viral pneumonia usually resolves by itself.

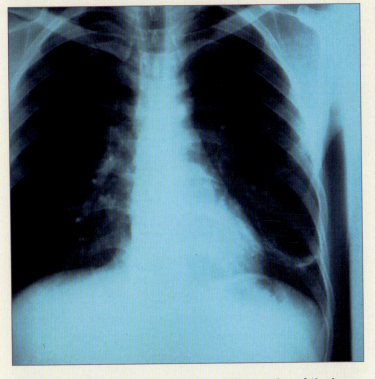

Figure 1.1 This chest X-ray shows an inflammation of the lungs caused by pneumonia.

Newspapers around the country picked up the story and the public immediately became concerned. The abruptness with which people had become ill, and the high number of deaths that occurred despite the illness being treated in big city medical center emergency rooms and receiving the most modern antibiotics, led to great concern.

Large outbreaks of disease that suddenly affect one place at one time call for an investigation by public health officials, including the federal Centers for Disease Control and Prevention (CDC), based in Atlanta, Georgia. Medical investigators went to Philadelphia and took environmental samples. Over a period of months, scientists identified the cause of the pneumonia outbreak at the American Legion convention as a previously unknown bacterium. It was given the name *Legionella pneumophila,* and the disease that this bacterium caused was given the name Legionnaires' disease or legionellosis.

Answering the question of what microorganism caused the disease outbreak in Philadelphia that summer was only one part—and the smaller part—of determining how and why the legionnaires and others had become ill. Where had this bacterium come from? Had it been in the food or the water? Had it been on the surfaces of tables, chairs, plates, or silverware?

Scientists conducted a thorough investigation of all the hotels where the convention had been held and where guests had stayed and determined that the bacterium had been living in one of the hotel's air conditioning systems. Whenever the air conditioning cycled on and the fans blew cold air throughout the building, *Legionella* bacteria traveled throughout the hotel's air ducts and into the rooms that were being cooled.

This made sense at the time, as the people who became ill all developed respiratory symptoms (although since then, medical researchers have come to believe that this is not always how *Legionella* makes people ill). If the bacteria had been in food or drinking water, it likely would have caused illnesses of the gastrointestinal tract because people would have ingested the bacteria when they ate, drank, or touched their fingers to their mouths. Because the bacteria had caused respiratory symptoms, it was most likely that it had been inhaled.

Because the legionnaires were a large crowd, they spent much of their time together in the hotel's ballroom. With all those people in one room in the middle of a Philadelphia summer, the air conditioning was usually running to keep the ballroom cool. The ductwork and air handling system became a primary suspect as the source of the bacteria, and that seemed to be borne from the research done by medical investigators.

Some medical investigators, however, were not convinced. If the bacteria had been **aerosolized** through the cooling

INVESTIGATING AN OUTBREAK

An outbreak of disease often leads to an investigation by public health authorities. These can be city, country, or state public health officials, or federal scientists and medical detectives from the federal Centers for Disease Control and Prevention (CDC) in Atlanta.

Public health investigations focus on getting to the root cause of a disease outbreak. If the illness is caused by a contagious **pathogen**, investigators determine who each person had been in contact with before he or she became ill and will find those people to see if they have been ill. In cases of illnesses that are not contagious, such as Legionnaires' disease, investigators test items that infected people have come in contact with to determine the pathogen's origin.

The CDC has sophisticated laboratories in which it can conduct tests of samples from sick individuals or the environment to try to determine what has made people ill.

ducts, why didn't many more people throughout the hotel become ill? Why was the illness so much more common among the middle-aged and elderly population of visiting legionnaires? Did the people who became ill have risk factors that others did not?

Over the next 30 years, these questions would come to be answered, and the picture we now have of Legionnaires' disease is very different than the picture the media painted in 1976.

TRACING *LEGIONELLA PNEUMOPHILA* BACKWARD AND FORWARD

Now that a new disease had been discovered, scientists went to work to see if this was the first outbreak or if this new microbe could possibly have been the cause of an earlier illness that had never been fully identified—which proved to be the case.

Legionella pneumophila was identified as being the cause of numerous earlier, usually much smaller, outbreaks of pneumonia and other respiratory illnesses dating back as far as 1957. Using stored serum samples from a 1965 outbreak of pneumonia at a psychiatric hospital in Washington D.C. that sickened 81 and killed 15, investigators were able to trace the cause to *Legionella.* Because many of these outbreaks had been small, and because the science of identifying new microbes had not begun to make great strides until the 1970s, scientists had not put the kind of effort into finding the cause of these other outbreaks that they put into finding the cause of the outbreak in Philadelphia in 1976.

The discovery of *Legionella pneumophila* in the evaporative cooler of one hotel in Philadelphia revolutionized public health. From that day on, the science and technology of water purification exploded into an enormous industry, and owners of apartment buildings, office buildings, hospitals, colleges and universities, and other large buildings with sophisticated heating, ventilation, and air conditioning (HVAC) systems sought to keep their equipment free of this deadly bacterium.

Things changed dramatically two years after the outbreak in Philadelphia. In 1978, medical investigators in the Veterans Administration Hospital System reviewed outbreaks of pneumonia over the previous four years at three Veterans Administration (VA) hospitals in Los Angeles, Pittsburgh, and Togus, Maine. They found that over 300 patients who developed pneumonia while in the hospital had been infected with *Legionella* bacteria, and that an astounding 50% of those infected with *Legionella* had died.

The VA patients who had become ill with *Legionella* infection had a number of risk factors for acute respiratory illness in common:

- Most were long-time cigarette smokers and many had chronic lung disease

- Some had received kidney transplants and were receiving **immunosuppressive drugs**

- Many had undergone some form of surgery that required general anesthesia, as well as placement of an endotracheal tube into the lungs to assist breathing while anesthetized

As had happened after the Philadelphia outbreak, when news of the VA outbreaks reached the public, many people, especially VA patients and staff in some hospitals, became fearful. In the Los Angeles VA hospital, *Legionella* outbreaks continued intermittently through 1982, with a total of 218 confirmed cases over the five-year period 1977–1982.

In the years since the initial investigation of Legionnaires' disease outbreaks in the late 1970s, more than 300 reports of hospital-acquired Legionnaires' disease have been reported by public health authorities or in peer-reviewed medical journals. In 2002, the CDC released a study of Legionnaires' disease cases from 1980 to 1998 that showed a total of 6,757 confirmed cases, or about 360 cases a year, in the United States. Legionnaires' disease has also been found in countries around the world. Most cases are diagnosed in the countries of the developed world, but scientists feel this is because Legionnaires' disease is simply not tested for in the less developed world, due to a lack of resources (Figure 1.2).

Research conducted in the 1980s and 1990s has determined that the primary source of the *Legionella* responsible for outbreaks in hospitals is not air conditioning cooling towers, but rather sources of **potable** water (tanks, pipes, and fixtures that hold and carry the water used for drinking, cooking, and bathing).

During that time, the science of **epidemiology** has also advanced greatly. Today, scientists and medical investigators can use the same kinds of "DNA fingerprinting" techniques used in criminal forensic science to understand how bacteria with the same DNA get from one place to another. Such molecular epidemiology has allowed researchers to differentiate among the various kinds of *Legionella* bacteria. It is now thought that *Legionella* bacteria of one sort or another exists in the potable water systems of most hospitals and other institutions, and even in the public drinking water systems of many cities. And it is thought by many scientists that most people, at one time or another, drink water contaminated with *Legionella*. Most people do not get sick, however, and of those who do get sick, most recover. Those who become most ill from *Legionella*, and are most likely to die from it, are those who are old or infirm.

Today, 30 years after the discovery of Legionnaires' disease, what do we know about it?

1. *Legionella pneumophilla*, the particular species of *Legionella* bacteria that causes Legionnaires' disease, is the most virulent of the *Legionella* forms.

2. *Legionella* is probably **endemic** to many public and institutional water supplies.

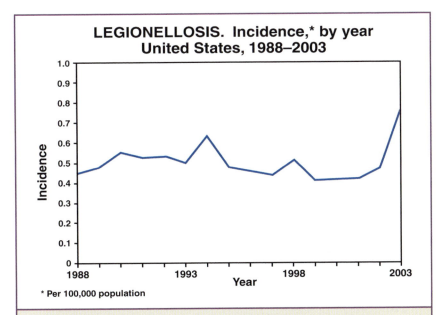

Figure 1.2 The increased incidence of legionellosis in 2003 was influenced largely by increases in the incidence of sporadic, community-aquired Legionnaires' disease in certain mid- and south Atlantic states. During this same period and in these same states, no changes occured in diagnostic methods, diagnostic test volume, or surveillance methods. These states did experience record levels of rainfall that correlated with the increased incidence of Legionnaires' disease; however, the precise nature of this association is unknown. Coutesy of CDC.

3. Many people become ill from *Legionella* but most recover. Those most likely to die of the disease are already compromised by weakened immune systems or chronic lung disease.

4. Many hospital deaths due to pneumonia may be linked to *Legionella,* but unless there is a reason to suspect an outbreak most hospitals do not test for it, especially in the deaths of chronically ill or terminally ill patients.

Legionella is not the plague it was thought to be 30 years ago when it was first discovered. Nevertheless, *Legionella* is a continuing public health concern that can be mitigated by hospitals, schools, and other institutions being vigilant about decontaminating their potable water sources and investigating *Legionella* as a possible source of illness when outbreaks occur.

2

Legionella Pneumophila

Since its discovery as the cause of an outbreak of pneumonia in Philadelphia in 1976, the bacterium that causes Legionnaires' disease (*Legionella pneumophila*) has been shown to be only one of many forms of *Legionella* bacteria. As of 2005, scientists had discovered 48 species and over 70 serotypes of the bacteria family Legionellaceae. Half of these bacteria have been implicated in illness in humans.

Over 90% of the known *Legionella*-related illness in humans is caused by a single species of the bacteria, *Legionella pneumophila*. This can be narrowed down even further: by far the most frequent culprit in human illness is *L. pneumophila* serotype 1. Since 1986, scientists have been able to break down these serotypes even further using **monoclonal antibodies**. Today, it is possible for public health researchers to determine where and how patients became infected by matching the monoclonal antibody subtypes in the patients' laboratory samples with those present in environmental samples.

We say "known illness" because, although experts at the CDC believe there are anywhere from 8,000 to 18,000 cases of *Legionella*-related illness of one form or another each year in the United States, the vast majority of cases are mild and go unreported. Also, although doctors are supposed to report known or suspected cases of Legionnaires' disease to their state departments of health, which in turn report to the CDC, it is believed that many suspected cases go unreported.

The CDC estimates are epidemiological projections based on **retro-spective** (after the fact) **studies.** By the time these studies are undertaken, usually only medical records are available; there are no specimen samples that can be tested to prove the presence of Legionnaires' disease. Therefore, the CDC says it "suspects" Legionnaires' disease while it is not able to verify or confirm that diagnosis through actual evidence.

Legionnaires' disease usually appears in clusters. In clusters that occur in a community rather than in a particular hospital, the first hint that Legionnaires' disease is occurring is an unusually large number of hospital admissions due to pneumonia.

Most cases of pneumonia are simply treated **symptomatically** and the underlying cause never becomes a concern. When large numbers of patients with pneumonia begin appearing in a small period of time, however, hospital personnel often begin testing samples of **sputum** (samples of fluid coughed up from the lungs) or blood from those patients. If *L. pneumophila* is discovered in these samples, the local or state health department usually alerts all hospitals in the area and emergency room personnel are encouraged to test everyone who comes to their hospitals with pneumonia. Sometimes the CDC becomes involved to help the local or state authorities conduct a thorough study of the situation.

LEGIONELLA THROUGH THE MICROSCOPE

Legionella bacteria are extremely small, measuring about 1/3 to 1 micron in width and 2 microns in length. They are rod shaped (Figure 2.1).

Legionella is a gram-negative bacterium, meaning that it is visible during the "counterstaining" portion of the **Gram staining process**. It grows in a laboratory using a buffered charcoal yeast extract agar, a process that usually takes 4 to 5 days. When grown on such a medium, *Legionella* colonies appear off-white and more rounded than rod-shaped (Figure 2.2). Identification of *Legionella* can also be made using the **direct fluorescent antibody (DFA) test** (Figure 2.3).

L. pneumophila is classified as a **facultative** intracellular **pathogen**. A pathogen is a microorganism that causes illness.

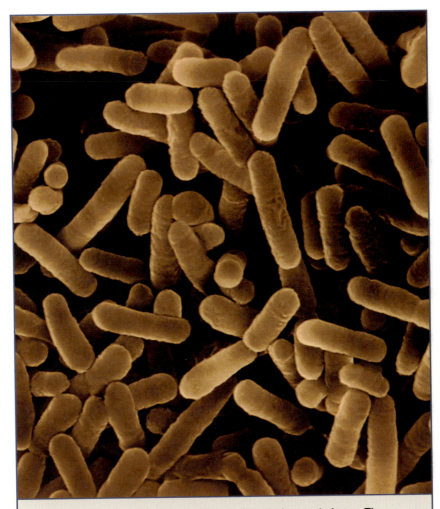

Figure 2.1 *Legionella* bacteria show a distinct rod shape. The rods are about 2 microns long by 1/2 to 1 micron wide.

"Facultative" means that the pathogen can adapt to different conditions; "intracellular" means that it lives within cells. *Legionella* infects and multiplies within, and eventually destroys, **macrophage** cells. Macrophages are cells that surround, engulf, and digest cellular debris (dead cells or pieces of destroyed cells) within the body.

HOW *LEGIONELLA* CAUSES INFECTION

Legionalla multiplies inside the host's cells until the cells rupture, which frees the new bacterial cells to infect other macrophages. In other words, *Legionella* makes people ill by destroying the very cells that help the immune system get rid of the debris that collects after the immune system does its work. This explains why people with weakened immune systems (people who are said to be **immunosuppressed** or **immunocompromised**) are especially vulnerable to Legionnaires' disease.

GRAM STAINING

In the late 19th century, Hans C. J. Gram, a Danish doctor born in 1853, developed a method for categorizing bacteria. The process is called Gram staining, and it is still used to this day.

First, a violet stain is put on the organism in question, followed by an iodine solution. The next step is to decolorize the sample using an alcohol or acetone solution. Finally, a safranin (synthetic dye) counterstain is placed on the sample. If the specimen retains the violet color of the original stain, the sample is said to be Gram-positive. If it retains the pink color of the counterstain, it is said to be Gram-negative.

Escherichia coli, *Salmonella*, and *Shigella*, three forms of bacteria that primarily attack the gastrointestinal tract, are all Gram-negative, as is *Legionella*. The bacteria that cause such divergent diseases as leprosy, tuberculosis, and common strep infections are all Gram-positive.

In the century since Gram developed his method of classification, pharmaceutical companies have developed antibiotic drugs that specifically target either Gram-negative or Gram-positive bacteria.

Figure 2.2 This *Legionella* colony was grown in a buffering charcoal yeast extract agar. *Legionella* colonies appear off-white and more rounded than rod-shaped.

LEGIONELLA'S SPECIAL
RELATIONSHIP WITH THE LUNGS

Legionella bacteria are cleared from the respiratory system through **mucociliary action**. The tiny hair-like **cilia** that line the inside of the respiratory organs—the nose, throat, larynx,

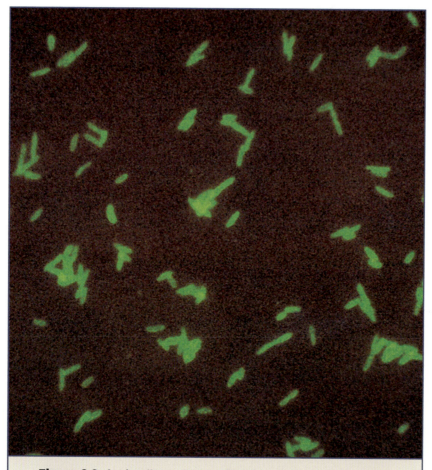

Figure 2.3 *Legionella* can be identified by using direct flourescent antibody (DFA) technology. Flourescent dye glows when *Legionella* are present.

trachea, bronchi, and lungs—move the bacteria up and out of the respiratory tract. Many healthy people probably become infected with *Legionella* but do not become ill because their respiratory systems work well and clear the bacteria before it can cause infection.

On the other hand, people with chronic respiratory illnesses, such as chronic obstructive pulmonary disease or chronic bronchitis, have respiratory systems that are damaged and thus not able to clear the bacteria. This is also true of people who inhale tobacco smoke, especially those who smoke cigarettes. This makes them more vulnerable to becoming ill if they are infected by *Legionella*.

LEGIONELLA IS ALL AROUND US

Many species of *Legionella* (though not *L. pneumophila)* have been found in freshwater environments such as ponds and streams, and the bacteria are thought to be endemic to fresh water throughout the world.

L. pneumophila, on the other hand, does not seem to occur in natural water sources. Rather, it tends to form, collect, and reproduce in contained areas where there is warm, stagnant water (between 90° and 105° Fahrenheit). Such water can be found in heating systems, hot-water-producing tanks for potable water, outside water tanks atop buildings in cities, cooling towers and evaporative condensers for large industrial air conditioning systems, and whirlpool spas. *L. pneumophila* also colonizes smaller environments that store warm water, such as humidifiers, respiratory therapy equipment, the equipment used to clean metal surgical tools, and even the reservoirs of ultrasonic machines that moisten the produce in supermarkets.

One species of *Legionella*, *L. longbeachae,* has been found in commercially produced potting soil and has been implicated in small outbreaks of human illness. (See case study)

In summary, *Legionella* is easily identified using conventional laboratory processes and easily categorized into types that cause human illness and types that do not. Although it is endemic to many naturally occurring freshwater environments, the *Legionella* species that causes most human illness is not found in such environments, but rather in man-made environments that collect water for industrial, commercial, or personal use.

CASE STUDY:
Legionella in Potting Soil

On June 13, 2000, health officials in Washington state alerted the Centers for Disease Control and Prevention (CDC) of a 46-year-old woman hospitalized with pneumonia who had been diagnosed with Legionnaires' disease. The strain of the disease was unusual; it was not caused by *L. pneumophila*, which is responsible for 90% of all cases of Legionnaires' disease in humans. Rather, the species of the bacteria responsible for the woman's pneumonia was *L. longbeachae*.

An interview with the woman about her activities in the 10 days prior to seeking medical treatment determined that she had been potting plants. A sample of the patient's sputum, as well as samples from two bags of potting soil and one bag of compost from her home, were all sent to the CDC for examination.

One of the bags of potting soil contained *L. longbeachae*. The compost contained other species of *Legionella*, but not *L. longbeachae*.

A month prior to this incident, the CDC had received two isolates of *L. longbeachae* from a 77-year-old Oregon woman and a 45-year-old California man.

These were the first reported incidents in the United States of infection with *L. longbeachae* from soil products. Reports from Japan and Australia had shown more frequent infection, and in Australia 33 of 45 potting soil samples in one test were positive for *Legionella* bacteria, with 26 samples containing *L. longbeachae*.

From 1990 to 1999, only 37 cases of infection with *L. longbeachae* had been reported to the CDC's *Legionella* reporting system. The 2,000 cases, although they occurred in rapid succession, were not the beginning of a major outbreak of illness. *L. longbeachae* continues to be an infrequent cause of illness in the United States.

3

A Difficult Diagnosis

A person infected with *Legionella pneumophila* who arrives at a doctor's office or hospital emergency room has symptoms similar to those of many other illnesses. These include fever, chills, fatigue, and muscle aches. Some people have respiratory symptoms—a cough that may be dry or may produce sputum, and possibly even chest pain when breathing or coughing. This makes Legionnaires' disease difficult to diagnose in its earliest stages.

A diagnosis of Legionnaires' disease is not technically difficult to make. But it necessitates laboratory tests that most doctors, and most emergency rooms, do not routinely administer. If the person is not having any chest pain, and if the doctor does not hear any breath sounds that hint at pneumonia, in many instances the doctor treats initial symptoms with **palliative care** (rest, fluid, and medication to reduce fever). If pneumonia is present or develops—as evidenced by examination with a stethoscope and a chest X-ray—the pneumonia is often treated with a broad-spectrum antibiotic, without the doctor taking blood or sputum samples for laboratory analysis.

If a person appears in a doctor's office or hospital emergency room with more extensive neurological or gastrointestinal (GI) symptoms, more sophisticated laboratory tests may be ordered. Neurological symptoms that may occur with Legionnaires' disease include lethargy, confusion, agitation, or, in extreme cases, stupor. GI symptoms include nausea, vomiting, watery (but not bloody) diarrhea, and abdominal pain.

Most public health doctors and scientists who examine outbreaks of Legionnaires' disease use the same standards for determining "definitive" and "probable" cases of the illness. A definitive diagnosis of Legionnaires' disease requires:

- Symptoms consistent with Legionnaires' disease

- A chest X-ray showing a patchy white pattern, usually bilateral (affecting both lungs) or multi-lobar (affecting more than one lobe in one lung)

- At least one of the following:

  ♦ Bacteria from a sputum sample that grow on culture medium

  ♦ Showing that the bacterium is present by using an immunoflourescent stain in the sputum sample of a living patient or on lung tissue at autopsy of someone who has died

  ♦ A fourfold or greater increase in antibody levels (known as **titers**) in two blood samples, one taken during the acute phase of illness and a second taken 3 to 4 weeks later

  ♦ A positive *Legionella* urinary antigen test

The urinary antigen test was not available until the late 1990s. Today it is the test used most frequently to confirm a diagnosis of Legionnaires' disease. The test can be done rapidly and is far less costly than other more complex laboratory methods of making the diagnosis.

Assays based on the **polymerase chain reaction (PCR)** can be used to get very specific information about the DNA in *Legionella*. This test is useful for epidemiologists, but less useful for doctors treating their patients. However, if other tests come back negative for *L. pneumophila*, this test can be useful in diagnosing illness caused by one of the other strains of *Legionella*.

COMMUNITY-ACQUIRED OR
HOSPITAL-ACQUIRED *LEGIONELLA*

Legionella is estimated to be the cause of up to 15% of all community-acquired cases of pneumonia requiring hospitalization, and the second most frequent cause of pneumonia requiring care in a hospital intensive care unit (ICU). *Legionella* is also thought be the cause of as much as 30% of all hospital-acquired pneumonia.

The incubation period for Legionnaires' disease generally varies from 2 to 10 days, but has been known to be as much as 15 days. This is another factor that makes investigating an outbreak of Legionnaires' disease difficult.

Once Legionnaires' disease is suspected to be the cause of a handful of cases of pneumonia, public health officials usually jump into action fairly quickly and conduct an investigation using a case-control methodology (Figure 3.1).

LEGIONNAIRES' DISEASE IN THE COMMUNITY

Outbreaks of Legionnaires' disease in the community generally occur when individuals inhale water vapor contaminated by *Legionella*. In various outbreaks investigated by public health authorities in the United States and around the world, this contamination has been shown to come from such disparate sources as industrial air conditioner cooling towers, whirlpool spas, and even an ultrasonic grocery store produce department "fog" machine. (See Case Study)

LEGIONNAIRES' DISEASE IN THE HOSPITAL

Outbreaks of Legionnaires' disease in hospital settings usually occur when patients with compromised immune systems aspirate (breathe in) water from the hospital's potable water system that is contaminated with *Legionella*.

Aspiration occurs when small amounts of water escape the gag reflex and go down the trachea instead of the esophagus.

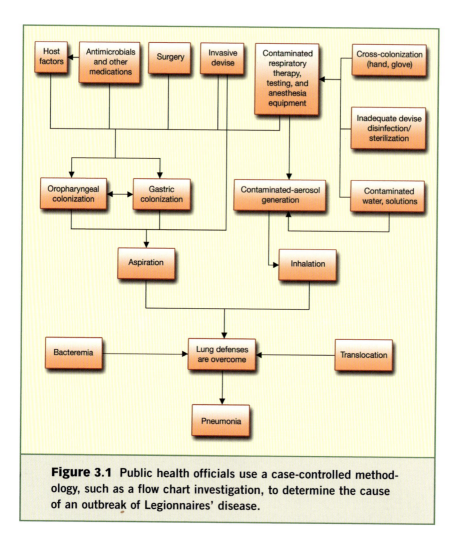

Figure 3.1 Public health officials use a case-controlled methodology, such as a flow chart investigation, to determine the cause of an outbreak of Legionnaires' disease.

This can occur while drinking, showering, or rinsing after brushing teeth.

After a hospital-based outbreak of Legionnaires' disease, the hospital usually investigates all of the fittings for the potable water system that people might come into contact with (water fountain heads, shower heads, and faucets) and often finds *Legionella* contamination at these sources, as well as in the hot water tank. Usually, the hospital changes the contaminated fittings and treats the water tank and hospital plumbing system either by superheating the hot water for a short period of time, or by superchlorinating the entire water system, both of which have been shown to be effective in killing *Legionella* (Table 3.1) (see Chapter 7).

Table 3.1 Risk factors and suggested infection-control measures.

Legionnaires' Disease/ Risk Factors	Suggested Infection-control Measures
HOST-RELATED	
Immunosuppression	Decrease duration of immunosuppression.
DEVICE-RELATED	
Contaminated aerosol from devices	Sterilize/disinfect aerosol-producing devices before use; use only sterile water for respiratory humidifying devices; do not use cool-mist room-air humidifiers without adequate sterilization or disinfection.
ENVIRONMENT-RELATED	
Aerosols from contaminated water supply	Hyperchlorinate or superheat hospital water system; routinely clean water-supply system; consider use of sterile water for drinking by immunosuppressed patients.
Cooling-tower draft	Properly design, place, and maintain cooling towers.

CASE-CONTROL EPIDEMIOLOGICAL STUDIES

In a case-controlled epidemiological study, public health investigators compare the experiences of a group of people who have become ill with a comparable group of people who have not become ill.

CASE-CONTROL EPIDEMIOLOGICAL STUDIES (*continued*)

For instance, one particular hospital in a community has diagnosed 20 cases of Legionnaires' disease in a 2-month period. This is clearly unusual. State public health officials decide to investigate and see if they can find a common source of infection for the 20 people.

The investigators go to the hospital and get the names of the 20 people who have developed Legionnaires' disease. For each patient, they also get the names of two people who have visited the emergency room for other reasons. These people, known as "healthy controls," are matched with the study subjects according to age, where they live, underlying diseases, whether or not they smoke cigarettes, and other relevant demographics.

The public health officials then conduct interviews with the 20 study subjects and the 40 control subjects. They ask the 60 people about what they did, where they went, and with whom they spent time in the 15 days prior to their emergency room visits.

Through such detailed interviews, public health officials are usually able to pinpoint a source of contamination that is common among all of the study subjects. In the case studies that follow throughout this book, you will read detailed stories of case-controlled epidemiological studies into Legionnaires' disease outbreaks that have occurred throughout the world.

CASE STUDY:
The Supermarket Fogger

On October 31, 1989, two doctors in the small city of Bogalusa, Louisiana (population 16,000), reported to the state's Department of Health and Hospitals that they had treated more than 50 cases of acute pneumonia in the previous 3 weeks. All of the patients were adults, and six had died.

Over the next 2 weeks, state health authorities confirmed 33 cases of Legionnaires' disease in patients hospitalized for acute pneumonia between October 10 and November 13 (Table 3.2). *L. pnuemophila* serotype 1 (Lp1) was confirmed by direct fluorescent antibody tests of lung tissue from two of the patients who had died.

In the previous 3 years, pneumonia admissions to "Hospital A" had tended to peak in January and February, with about 20 to 25 cases per month. But in 1989, 70 patients were admitted to "Hospital A" in October, compared with an average of 11 cases in October in the previous 3 years.

The Centers for Disease Control and Prevention (CDC) in Atlanta sent epidemiological investigation officers to assist the state health department in its investigation. The investigators

	1986	1987	1988	1989
January	12	20	21	16
February	14	19	26	19
March	7	21	8	27
April	12	10	11	13
May	?	?	?	?
June	4	11	11	6
July	5	5	9	8
August	6	9	12	7
September	6	7	13	8
October	15	8	10	70
November	?	8	11	?
December	?	11	20	?
TOTAL	75	129	153	174

Table 3.2 Number of patients diagnosed with pneumonia discharged from Hospital A, by Month, January 1986–October 1989. Courtesy of CDC.

CASE STUDY:
The Supermarket Fogger (*continued*)

enrolled 28 pneumonia patients and 56 health controls in a case-controlled study, and interviewed them extensively about their exposure to potential sources of *Legionella*. They focused on industrial cooling towers, which in 1989 were thought to be the most likely source of *Legionella* contamination (Table 3.3).

Extensive interviews showed very little variation between patients and controls in their exposure—either indoor or outdoor—to buildings with cooling towers. The one major difference in exposure was at a grocery store where many of the study subjects said they shopped.

Although half of the healthy controls had been to the grocery store, nearly all (93%) of the pneumonia patients had been to the grocery store in the days before they became ill. On further interviewing, these patients told investigators that their time in the store was greater than the time spent in the store by the healthy controls.

After getting the permission of the grocery store manager, investigators found the source of aerosolized water, a "fogger" machine in the produce section. Unlike conventional produce-misting machines, which intermittently spray a fine mist from a hose, the machine in question used ultrasonic technology and a reservoir of warm water (similar to a home ultrasonic humidifier) to produce a continuous fine-mist "fog."

The investigators cultured the reservoir and found Lp1 present. They dismantled the machine and shipped it to the CDC, which under laboratory conditions produced fog that was also contaminated with Lp1. The grocery store chain stopped using the technology, as did most others in the industry, after the results of the Bogalusa outbreak were made public.

A number of the grocery store employees who agreed to blood tests were shown to have elevated antibodies to *Legionella*, meaning they had been infected but had not been made ill.

	Cases Exposed/Total (%)		Cases Exposed/Total (%)		Odds Ratio	P-value
INDOOR EXPOSURE TO BUILDINGS WITH COOLING TOWERS						
Retail Store A	3/28	(11%)	10/54	(19%)	0.5	0.5
Post Office	7/27	(26%)	12/50	(24%)	1.1	0.9
Hospital A	5/28	(18%)	12/54	(22%)	0.8	0.9
Hospital B	3/28	(11%)	7/56	(13%)	0.8	1.0
Paper Mill	2/28	(7%)	4/56	(7%)	1.0	1.0
OUTDOOR EXPOSURE TO STORES NEAR PAPER MILL COOLING TOWERS						
Retail Store A	3/28	(11%)	10/54	(19%)	0.5	0.5
Retail Store B	10/28	(36%)	15/52	(29%)	1.4	0.7
Retail Store D	5/28	(18%)	7/54	(13%)	1.5	0.5
Retail Store E	6/28	(21%)	9/54	(17%)	1.4	0.8
Restaurant A	2/26	(8%)	5/52	(10%)	0.8	1.0
Bank A	11/28	(39%)	19/53	(36%)	1.2	0.9
Butcher Store A	12/27	(44%)	10/54	(19%)	3.5	0.03
Any of the above	19/28	(68%)	33/56	(59%)	1.5	0.6
OUTDOOR EXPOSURE TO OTHER LARGE COOLING TOWERS						
Drug Store A	7/28	(25%)	15/55	(27%)	0.9	1.0
Drug Store B	13/28	(46%)	20/54	(37%)	1.5	0.6
Doctors Plaza A	2/27	(7%)	8/56	(14%)	0.5	0.5
Retail Store F	4/28	(14%)	6/54	(11%)	1.3	0.7
EXPOSURE TO STORES FREQUENTLY REPORTED BY CASE-PATIENTS						
Grocery Store A	25/27	(93%)	28/54	(52%)	11.6	<0.01
Grocery Store B	19/28	(68%)	23/54	(43%)	2.9	0.05
Retail Store C	22/28	(79%)	30/54	(56%)	2.9	0.07

Table 3.3 Exposures to buildings, Legionnaires' disease outbreak, Louisiana, 1989. Courtesy of CDC.

CASE STUDY:
Legionnaires' Disease in and Around New York City in 2005

In July 2005, the New York State Department of Health issued new guidelines for hospitals to decontaminate their water supplies. The rules were issued in response to outbreaks of Legionnaires' disease in New York City and in suburban Westchester County in the previous few months. Another Manhattan hospital had detected the presence of *Legionella*

CASE STUDY:
Legionnaires' Disease in and
Around New York City in 2005 (continued)

pneumophila in its water system after the first outbreak, although no illnesses had been attributed to the contamination.

The new regulations require any hospital that has detected *Legionella* in its water supply to test for it and decontaminate its water supply every 6 months, whether or not the bacteria are found on the semi-annual tests. Hospitals with transplant units must test and decontaminate regardless of the test outcome every 3 months.

Hospitals that have not had an outbreak and do not have transplant units—by far the majority of hospitals in the state—are under no obligation to test and decontaminate until their first outbreak occurs. This has led experts to contend that intermittent outbreaks of Legionnaires' disease will continue to plague New York hospitals, as it does in many other parts of the country.

Dr. Victor Yu, Chief of Infectious Diseases at the Pittsburgh Veterans Administration Health Center and a world-renowned expert on Legionnaires' disease, estimates that *Legionella* is present in the water supplies of up to 70% of American hospitals, in at least trace amounts. "The public only hears about the hospitals that have the ability to find it in their drinking water," Dr. Yu told *The New York Times* on May 1, 2005.

The New York outbreaks of 2005 were different, in that one was traced to the hospital's potable water system, whereas the other was traced to an air conditioning cooling tower near the hospital's emergency room door.

In late March and early April, four patients at New York Presbyterian/Columbia hospital, in the far northwest corner of Manhattan, fell ill with suspected Legionnaires' disease. Two patients eventually died, and the diagnoses were confirmed on autopsy. The incidents became public only at the beginning of May. The hospital had already decontaminated the water supply throughout the hospital campus.

The day the hospital announced the outbreak, it also made public that after the outbreak it had tested the water supply at its other Manhattan campus, about 5 miles away in the Upper East Side neighborhood. *Legionella* had been found in one building on that campus, although no cases of the illness had been attributed to that contamination.

Harlem Hospital, about one mile away from the New York Presbyterian campus where the four patients had become ill, also discovered traces of *Legionella* on a showerhead and faucet in its patient building around the same time, and decontaminated its water supply as well.

The second New York outbreak occurred about 20 miles north of New York City, at the Sound Shore Medical Center, a small hospital in New Rochelle in Westchester County. On July 14, 2005, the county health commissioner and the hospital announced that at least nine people had been diagnosed with Legionnaires' disease since June 21, 2005. All had previously come to the hospital as outpatients and had entered the hospital through the same door, which is near an industrial air conditioning cooling tower. By July 21, the number of confirmed cases had risen to 18. All had been treated for Legionnaires' disease either as outpatients or briefly as inpatients, and all were recovering.

Typically, Westchester County sees 7 to 10 cases of Legionnaires' disease each year, according to Dr. Joshua Lipsman, the county health commissioner. Dr. Lipsman suggested that the cooling tower, which tested negative for *Legionella* in the spring, may have become contaminated because of the humid weather and heavy rains that occurred in New York during June, both of which promote bacteria growth.

4

It's in the Water

Today, 30 years after the discovery of Legionnaires' disease, it is believed that many cases—especially those that occur inside hospitals—are caused not by inhaling aerosolized *Legionella,* but rather by aspirating water contaminated by *Legionella.* This is an important distinction.

While we all inhale, we do not all aspirate. We inhale every time we take a breath, and if bacteria were airborne in an aerosolized form, it would endanger anyone who is inhaling the contaminated air. Aspiration is taking material into the lungs that should be going down the esophagus into the stomach. Aspiration is usually caused by choking.

If the potable water supply of a hospital or other institutional setting—such as a prison or university dormitory—is contaminated, everyone who lives or works there is susceptible to becoming infected with *Legionella.* The big question then becomes, why do certain people become ill while most do not? The answer, according to doctors and scientists, has to do with underlying disease and the reason for hospitalization.

In June 2002, the British medical journal *The Lancet* published a review article about hospital-acquired Legionnaires' disease by Drs. Miquel Sabria and Victor Yu. Dr. Sabria is associated with a major transplant hospital in Barcelona, Spain. Dr. Yu, a world-renowned expert on Legionnaires' disease, is Chief of the Infectious Disease Section at the Veterans Administration Medical Center in Pittsburgh, Pennsylvania, and a consultant to hospitals around the country on controlling and mitigating Legionnaires' disease outbreaks.

Dr. Sabria and Dr. Yu reviewed the 25-year history of medical detection of Legionnaires' disease and the changing theories about what causes hospital-acquired outbreaks. Although case-control studies of community outbreaks have consistently found that most are due to inhalation of aerosolized *Legionella* from industrial water-cooling systems, the situation in hospitals is far different.

FALSE STARTS:
FROM COOLING TOWERS TO PATIENT SHOWERS

When the first outbreaks of Legionnaires' disease were identified in hospitals in the late 1970s and early 1980s—after the Philadelphia hotel outbreak that gave the disease its name—it was believed that air conditioning cooling towers were always to blame. Investigators from the CDC were often able to find a cooling tower in the hospital's vicinity that was colonized with *Legionella*, and usually theorized that wind had blown the aerosolized bacteria toward the hospital, which then sucked the bacteria in through its ventilation system.

But between 1982 and 1985, this theory fell apart. Close epidemiological investigation of hospital-acquired Legionnaires' disease showed that in many cases patients who became ill were in wings of the hospital that were not only far from the suspect cooling towers, but that used ventilation systems that could not have been affected by airborne aerosolized bacteria.

Some researchers suspected that the hospitals' own potable water systems were being colonized by the bacteria, and investigations into that possibility began. As Drs. Sabria and Yu write:

> From 1982 to 1985, the pivotal discovery was made that the potable water supply was the actual source of hospital-acquired Legionnaires' disease. Since this discovery, reported cases of hospital-acquired Legionnaires' disease linked to cooling towers have all but disappeared. It is noteworthy that of hundreds of hospital-acquired outbreaks since 1985, virtually all have been linked to potable water.

Three hospital outbreaks in the late 1980s were originally thought to be caused by cooling towers, but cases of

Legionnaires' disease continued to occur in the months after the cooling systems were decontaminated.

Once the aspiration theory caught hold in the mid-1980s, investigators began studying the problem from all different angles, and environmental technologists began exploring ways to decontaminate potable water supplies, all in the hopes of reducing the number of outbreaks of Legionnaires' disease among hospitalized patients. (See Chapter 7.)

Short of continuously decontaminating a hospital's water supply (even if no *Legionella* is found in random samples) or sampling 100% of every faucet and showerhead in the hospital, it is impossible to guarantee that *Legionella* is not present in a hospital's potable water supply. Researchers have therefore focused their efforts on limiting the exposure of patients, especially patients susceptible to aspiration of potentially contaminated water.

For a period of time, this meant not allowing post-surgical patients to shower, since in random sampling *Legionella* was often found on showerheads. Studies in the 1980s suggested a causal link between showering and developing Legionnaires' disease. More rigorous case-control studies of these outbreaks, however, eliminated showering as the cause of becoming ill. Today, doctors believe that post-surgical patients well enough to get out of bed and shower are much less susceptible to choking and aspirating, and therefore less likely to aspirate water infected with *Legionella* and to develop Legionnaires' disease than those who are not ambulatory.

UNDERLYING DISEASE A MAJOR INFLUENCE

Most people who contract Legionnaires' disease while hospitalized are very ill. Transplant patients, especially heart transplant patients, are the most likely to contract Legionnaires' disease. Anyone who has surgery that requires general anesthesia is at risk, although not to the same extent as transplant recipients.

The tubes used in **intubation**—when a patient is placed on a respirator to breathe during surgery or for another reason—have frequently been implicated in outbreaks of Legionnaires' disease. Nasogastric tubes—tubes that run through the nose and into the stomach to deliver nourishment or release pressure after abdominal surgery—have also been implicated. The theory is that in such cases the water used to sterilize the tubing is contaminated, the tubing is improperly dried after sterilization, and patients aspirate the contaminated water on the tubing.

Patients with chronic lung disease are also at higher risk than the general patient population, as are those who smoke cigarettes and those who have been treated with systemic corticosteroid medications, which cause changes in the body's immune system.

Patients infected with the human immunodeficiency virus (HIV), which causes acquired immune deficiency syndrome (AIDS) do not seem to be at higher risk than the general patient population for developing hospital-acquired Legionnaires' disease.

PROPER DIAGNOSIS IS KEY

Since the 1980s, better diagnosis and quicker treatment of hospital-acquired Legionnaires' disease has led to a dramatic drop in the number of patients who die from the disease. In the earliest reports of hospital outbreaks, in the late 1970s and early 1980s, upwards of 80% of patients who developed Legionnaires' disease died, which led to such panic that employees refused to come to work and families removed patients from hospitals.

Once the discovery was made that most cases of hospital-acquired Legionnaires' disease resulted from aspiration of contaminated water and not inhalation of vapors, the **mortality rate** (the percentage of ill people who actually die) declined rapidly, falling to around 46% by 1986 and all the way to 14% by 1998.

Today, the mortality rate for community-acquired Legionnaires' disease is higher than that for hospital-acquired disease.
This is most likely because of the time lag between when
people in the community become ill and when they are
diagnosed and treated.

Nevertheless, Legionnaires' disease continues to be under
diagnosed in hospitals. According to Dr. Sabria and Dr. Yu,
only 19% of U.S. hospitals that participate in CDC monitoring
of hospital-acquired pneumonia routinely test patients who
develop pneumonia for *Legionella,* and only 25% of hospitals
that have experienced cases of hospital-acquired Legionnaires'
disease routinely test patients who develop pneumonia after
the initial outbreak.

Dr. Yu has been among the most outspoken experts for
tighter standards for hospitals throughout America in their
efforts to reduce the incidence of hospital-acquired Legionnaires' disease. The Veterans Administration Medical Center
in Pittsburgh, where he works, has the tightest Legionnaires'
monitoring program in the country. Maryland has the
strictest regimen for systematically testing hospitals. After
the outbreaks of Legionnaires' disease at two New York
hospitals in the spring and summer of 2005, one in New
York City and the other in suburban Westchester County,
and the discovery of *Legionella* at another New York City
hospital, New York State tightened its regulations. (See
Chapter 3)

Legionella is "in the water," both in naturally occurring
water sources and in man-made water systems that provide
heating, cooling, and potable water for many institutions.
Most of us who inhale vapors from or drink water contaminated by *Legionella* will not become ill. However, people
with underlying medical conditions that make them susceptible to aspiration, those with underlying lung disease,
and those with compromised immune systems, continue to
be at risk.

CASE STUDY:
Over 400 Confirmed Legionnaires' Disease Cases in Murcia, Spain

On July 7, 2001, the Regional Health Council of Murcia, in southeastern Spain, was notified by local hospitals of an unusually high number of pneumonia cases. The number of hospital admissions for pneumonia had been growing since June 26, 2001, and had become alarming.

The council investigated the outbreak. By the end of the day on July 8, 2001, they had identified over 100 suspected cases of Legionnaires' disease. By July 22, two weeks after the onset of the outbreak and after the last cases had been treated, over 800 potential cases of Legionnaires' disease had been identified. At the end of the summer, when all of the retrospective analyses had been completed, the health council had confirmed 449 cases of Legionnaires' disease, the largest outbreak in history (Figures 4.1 and 4.2).

Hospital admission was necessary in 74% of the confirmed cases. Only 1.1% of the cases resulted in death, a remarkable statistic for a community outbreak. When the analysis was completed, this was shown to be due to the rapid response of health authorities, from hospital doctors to the regional health council, in identifying and treating those with the infection. Another factor contributing to the low mortality rate was the fact that fewer patients had predisposing health factors such as chronic lung disease and/or risk factors such as cigarette smoking.

Cases were confirmed by chest X-ray and laboratory tests. The health council made extensive use of urine antigen testing, a faster and more efficient method of detecting the presence of *Legionella* than traditional blood, sputum, or lung-tissue testing.

The health council developed an epidemiological questionnaire and interviewed those suspected of having Legionnaires'

CASE STUDY:
Over 400 Confirmed Legionnaires'
Disease Cases in Murcia, Spain (*continued*)

disease within 48 hours of their being treated in a hospital emergency room. The council created an extensive computer database to analyze these questionnaires, which dealt with clinical symptoms, predisposing health factors, risk factors, where people lived, and where they had traveled recently within the city.

This descriptive study showed no common indoor source of potential exposure, and suggested that an outdoor source

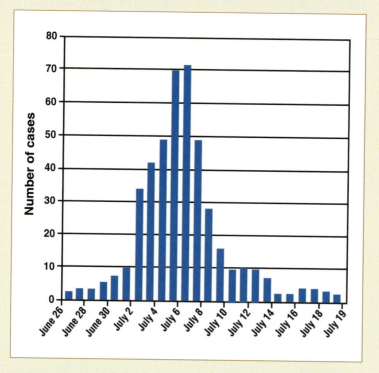

Figure 4.1 Confirmed cases of Legionnaires' disease by date of onset of illness, Murcia, Spain, June 26–July 19, 2001. Courtesy of *MMWR*, CDC.

in the northern part of the city was most likely to blame. An environmental investigation throughout the city resulted in a list of 339 installations, such as cooling towers, water storage tanks, and decorative street fountains that could harbor *Legionella*. Water samples were taken from some sites, which were chosen by analyzing the descriptive study. No *Legionella* was found in the city's drinking water supply or any fountains, but *L. pnuemophila* serotype 1 (Lp1) was found in 19 cooling towers and three 3-water-storage tanks.

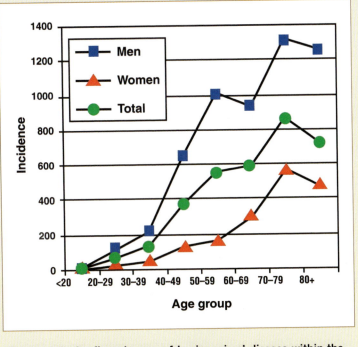

Figure 4.2 Confirmed cases of Legionnaires' disease within the city of Murcia, Spain. Specific incidence rates by sex and age (per 100,000). Courtesy of *MMWR*, CDC.

CASE STUDY:
Over 400 Confirmed Legionnaires'
Disease Cases in Murcia, Spain (continued)

A case-control study was established, using patients who lived outside of the city. A total of 85 cases and 170 healthy controls were enrolled in the study. Patients living outside of the city were chosen for two reasons. First, in some neighborhoods, there was a high incidence of Legionnaires' disease (more than 1%), which would have made sorting out potential causes difficult. Second, people living outside of the city would be more likely to remember specifically when they had been to the city, where they had gone, and other important details.

The case-control study discovered a strong association between traveling into the city within 2 weeks of falling ill and having a confirmed case of Legionnaires' disease. Almost all patients had traveled to the city, whereas fewer than half of the healthy controls had done so.

In addition, the patients had all been within a "zone of exposure" of one particular potential source. Zones of exposure were defined as one city block or a 200-meter circle. Although three other potential zones of exposure also showed a higher rate of illness by those who had "walked" through them (walking defined as actual walking or riding on an open scooter or bicycle as opposed to riding in a car or bus) using some statistical models, only one showed the higher incidence on all eight statistical models.

Ironically, the apparent cause of the outbreak was a cooling tower of a hospital. When tested, the cooling tower was found to be colonized with Lp1 of the same subtype as that seen in the patients, as determined by monoclonal antibody subtyping. Data from the local weather service showed that in the last days of June and the first days of July, high humidity, light winds, and an atmospheric inversion occurred, all of which have been shown to increase bacterial colonization in standing water.

As the community outbreak was occurring, the hospital with the cooling tower ultimately implicated also had an outbreak of hospital-acquired Legionnaires' disease, with 11 definite or likely cases occurring in a 2-week period. The hospital's water system was found to be free of *Legionella*, and it was suspected that the patients became infected by aerosolized bacteria from the cooling tower either upon entering the hospital or during their stay. This was the first time an outbreak caused by a hospital cooling tower had sickened already hospitalized patients.

As a result of the explosive outbreak in Murcia, within 20 days of the health council's final report in the fall of 2001, national legislation was passed in Spain concerning prevention and control of Legionnaires' disease outbreaks.

This was not the first outbreak of Legionnaires' disease associated with a hospital cooling tower. Over a 5-week period in April and May of 1985, 158 people were hospitalized with acute respiratory infections in Staffordshire, England. Of these patients, 101 people were eventually confirmed to have Legionnaires' disease, and 28 died.

A case-control study showed that the only commonality in the patients' lives over the 10 days prior to falling ill was to make a visit to the local hospital's outpatient clinics, which were located through the hospital entrance near an air-conditioning cooling tower. Most of those who died were elderly and had visited the outpatient department of the District General Hospital in the week following the long Easter weekend.

CASE STUDY:
Over 400 Confirmed Legionnaires'
Disease Cases in Murcia, Spain *(continued)*

In New Rochelle, a suburb of New York City, in 2005, 18 people were confirmed to have Legionnaires' disease caused by a cooling tower near a hospital entrance.

5

Complications from Legionnaires' Disease

Legionnaires' disease can be fatal. It is less often fatal today than it was 30 years ago, when the disease was discovered. This is due to better surveillance and faster public health responses to outbreaks, better diagnostic tools, and more targeted antibiotic therapies (See Chapter 6). Even in the Legionnaires' disease cases that are not fatal, however, there can be long-term lung, heart, kidney, liver, or neurological complications.

Once infection is established with any species of *Legionella* bacteria—certainly with *L. pneumophila*—pneumonia usually develops. In addition to the lungs, *Legionella* sometimes infects the lymph nodes, brain, kidney, liver, spleen, bone marrow, and the **myocardium** (the wall around the heart).

The most common **extrapulmonary** (outside the lungs) effects of Legionnaires' disease involve the heart; these include **myocarditis, pericarditis**, and prosthetic-valve **endocarditis**. In fact, heart-transplant patients and patients who have received a heart-valve replacement are among the most susceptible to developing hospital-acquired Legionnaires' disease. When this was first noticed, doctors theorized that heart-transplant and valve-replacement patients had weakened immune systems due to the immunosuppressive drugs they received, and were also prone to aspiration because of their generally weakened condition, which made them susceptible to developing Legionnaires' disease. In many cases of heart complications due to Legionnaires' disease that occur after open-heart surgery, however, there is no overt pneumonia. This odd fact has led researchers to suspect that

CASE STUDY:
Legionnaires' Disease on a Cruise Ship

On July 15, 1994, the New Jersey Department of Health noti-fied the Centers for Disease Control and Prevention (CDC) in Atlanta that six cases of pneumonia had been diagnosed in state residents who had recently traveled to Bermuda aboard the cruise ship *Horizon*.

Local, state, and federal health officials investigated. By August 10, 1994, a total of 14 individuals who had traveled on the *Horizon* between April 30 and July 9 and developed pneumonia within a couple of weeks had been diagnosed with Legionnaires' disease caused by *L. pneumophila* serotype 1 (Lp1). There were 28 other probable cases, although it was impossible to make definitive diagnoses in most cases because the illness had occurred in the spring and early summer and no blood, sputum, or urine samples were available for laboratory analysis.

A case-control study was performed, using patients and passengers who had traveled on the same cruises and not become ill. Health officials also conducted environmental sampling of the ship's water system. Use of the ship's whirlpool bath was strongly associated with developing Legionnaires' disease. Cultures taken from a sand filter used to recirculate whirlpool bath water yielded Lp1 with the same monoclonal antibody subtyping as that in the individuals who had developed Legionnaires' disease.

This outbreak was the first instance of Legionnaires' disease aboard a cruise ship docking at a U.S. port. It was not the first instance of Legionnaires' disease associated with whirlpool baths, nor would it be the last. The CDC held a symposium in the fall of 1994 to discuss Legionnaires' disease associated with whirlpool baths, and developed recommenda-tions for caring for whirlpool baths onboard ships to reduce the transmission of disease by this means.

Legionella is introduced into the chest cavity during the surgery by way of contaminated water. Foreign bodies such as chest tubes to drain fluid, or even the sutures used to close the wound, may have been contaminated by *Legionella*-tainted water in the hospital's potable water system.

This theory is supported by evidence of *Legionella* infection in other surgical wound sites. One patient has been reported with a **superinfection** of a surgical hip wound after being placed into a tub whose faucets were later found to be colonized with *L. pneumophila* serotype 1 (Lp1). Many other incidents of wound infection with *Legionella* have also been noted over the years.

This was one of the facts that for many years led hospitals to not allow their transplant and other surgical patients to

(continued on page 53)

CASE STUDY:
Legionnaires' Disease in a Virginia Home Improvement Store

Sometimes, it isn't even necessary to take a bath to become ill from a whirlpool.

On October 15, 1996, local health officials in southeastern Virginia contacted the Virginia Health Department about an unusual cluster of 15 patients admitted to a local hospital with pneumonia of unknown origin in the previous 2 days. On October 21, another hospital 15 miles away notified the state health authorities that its pneumonia census had taken an unusual upward turn in the first 2 weeks of the month before declining. On October 23, the local health district was notified of three confirmed cases of Legionnaires' disease among residents who lived in the district; one patient was committed to the hospital that had made the first report and the other two residents were at hospitals outside of the district.

CASE STUDY:
Legionnaires' Disease in a Virginia
Home Improvement Store (continued)

The state health authorities asked all hospitals and health providers in the area for medical records of anyone treated for pneumonia from September 1 through November 12, 1996. They also asked for sputum, blood, or urine samples for as many of those patients as possible.

Eventually, 23 confirmed cases of infection with *L. pneumophila* serotype 1 (Lp1) were identified among area residents. Of these 23 patients, two died (9.5% mortality).

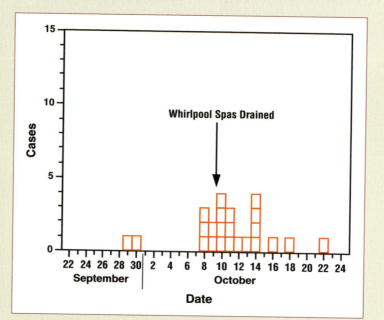

Number of cases of Legionnaires' disease*, by date of onset— Virginia, September–October 1996[†]. Courtesy of *MMWR*, CDC.

* Pneumonia in an area resident with onset of illness during September– November 12 with *Legionella pneumophilia* serogroup 1 identified by culture of sputum, antigen assay of urine, or fourfold rise in serum antibody titers.

[†] n–23.

A case-control study using 15 patients and 30 healthy controls was conducted to determine potential exposure. Of the 15 patients, 14 reported visiting a large home improvement center during the 2 weeks before they became ill; 12 control subjects also visited the store.

The cumulative average time in the store was 79 minutes for patients as opposed to 29 minutes for controls. In addition, 10 patients reported spending significant time in the store around the whirlpool spas, compared with three controls. The other four patients, and one control, reported "walking by" the spa display.

No other exposure, including drinking from the water fountain in the store or passing one of 14 other locations in the community designated as potential sources of *Legionella*, were associated with illness.

Samples were taken throughout the home improvement store and cultured to determine the presence of *L. pneumophila*. Among the items tested were the whirlpool spa basins and fixtures, spa filters, the sprinkler system in the greenhouse, a decorative fish pond and fountain, water fountains, and urinals, toilets, and faucets in the restrooms. In addition, the filter from a second whirlpool spa that had been sold, drained, and shipped to a customer, was tested, and health officials visited the purchaser's home to test the spa itself.

In all, three spa filters were tested. One had been used with the spa that was sold on October 11. The other two had been used with the spa that was still in the store, but that had been drained and was not running from October 9 through October 17.

The filter from the spa that was sold tested positive for Lp1 of the same subtype as that found in two patients, as

CASE STUDY:
Legionnaires' Disease in a Virginia
Home Improvement Store (*continued*)

determined by monoclonal antibody subtyping, and was determined to be the source of the *Legionella* contamination.

Three things are interesting and important about this occurrence. It was the first time people had contracted Legionnaires' disease from a whirlpool without actually entering the tub. In previous cases involving whirlpool spas, aspiration of small amounts of contaminated water could have easily been the case. However, here it is clear that inhalation of aerosolized *Legionella* from the contaminated filter was the cause of illness.

Second, this was one of the few times that an incidence of community-acquired Legionnaires' disease occurred from an indoor airborne source. Most other cases of inhalation-induced *Legionella* had occurred from outdoor sources such as cooling towers and water towers. Of course, the original outbreak that led to the discovery of Legionnaires' disease occurred indoors, in a Philadelphia hotel, in 1976, and on rare instances since then an air conditioning system has been determined to be the culprit of an outbreak.

Third, one of the 15 patients in the case-control study was infected with a different subtype of Lp1, and had no exposure to the home improvement store. Had there not been an outbreak of Legionnaires' disease due to a single source in the same region at the time that this patient became ill, his or her illness would most likely never have been diagnosed as Legionnaires' disease, because most hospitals do not routinely test pneumonia cases for evidence of *Legionella*. The source that made this patient ill was never found, but the patient was able to receive immediate treatment because Legionnaires' disease was diagnosed in a timely manner.

(continued from page 49)

shower, for fear of their wounds becoming infected with *Legionella* from a contaminated shower head. Over time, this policy has changed, as most doctors believe that far more cases of Legionnaires' disease are contracted by surgical patients through aspiration than through wound infection.

Even patients who recover from acute *Legionella* infection may continue to suffer from long-term lung damage, neurological changes, or other effects.

6

Treatment

Research has shown that prompt and appropriate care for Legionnaires' disease is important if a patient is to recover. Emergency room and primary care doctors are increasingly becoming educated to the need for a high degree of suspicion that a patient is infected with *Legionella* if he or she presents the following symptoms:

- Pneumonia with extrapulmonary symptoms such as diarrhea, lack of urine output, and neurological symptoms such as severe headache or confusion

- **Hyponatremia** (lower than normal concentration of salt in the body), a symptom of kidney failure that occurs because water is not excreted from the body, increasing the proportion of water to salt

CASE STUDY: Legionnaires' Disease in an Automotive Plant

Many different species of *Legionella* have been found in environmental samples taken from numerous industrial workplace settings over the years. Sources of contamination have included industrial fluids, potable water systems, and nozzle heads used with hoses for water-cooling production machinery in the factories or water-treatment plants where outbreaks have occurred.

Between March 11 and 15, 2001, four workers at an automotive engine manufacturing plant outside Cleveland,

Ohio, were diagnosed with Legionnaires' disease. Two of them died. They most likely had been exposed to *L. pneumophila* serotype 1 (Lp1) between March 2 and March 4.

There were no other confirmed cases, although nine other employees of the 2,500-worker plant were hospitalized between February 14 and March 28, four of them with pneumonia. Those four were listed as possible Legionnaires' disease cases.

The plant was shut down for a week in late March so health officials could take environmental samples. *Legionella* was isolated from 18 of 197 samples taken from the four areas of the 1.6 million square-foot manufacturing facility. As a result of these positive tests, the plant's entire potable water system was decontaminated, and a program of ongoing environmental surveillance for the presence of *Legionella* was initiated.

At least five species of *Legionella* were found in the samples. Three of those samples grew Lp1, but none matched the subtypes found in the patients when further tested by monoclonal antibody subtyping.

A case-control study was performed comparing the two living confirmed cases and the four possible cases against 12 healthy controls. Visiting one of the product finishing lines in the plant was associated with disease.

This is an example of a short-lived and transient colonization of a strain of *Legionella* leading to an outbreak of disease. However, had the outbreak not occurred, no environmental sampling would have taken place, and the plant's management would not have known that *Legionella* was present in the water supply. As so often is the case with Legionnaires' disease incidents, this was an outbreak waiting to happen.

- Gram-negative respiratory sample

- Positive urine antigen test (70% of infections test as true-positive results; there are few false-positive results)

In hospital settings, doctors are urged to suspect Legionnaires' disease in any case of hospital-acquired pneumonia.

Over the 30 years since Legionnaires' disease was discovered, doctors have refined the treatment, and new and more effective antibiotics have been discovered. The most common antibiotics used to treat Legionnaires' disease are in the families known as **macrolides, quinolones,** and **tetracyclines**. The drugs of choice are based on retrospective studies of what has worked in the past; there have been no **prospective studies** (studies in which patients are randomized and given one treatment or another to study the effectiveness). That is because Legionnaires' disease is a sudden-onset illness that tends to appear in outbreaks and can kill very quickly. In such a situation, experimentation just to learn how effective various medications are is not ethical; experimentation with new medications only occurs when patients are unresponsive to old treatments.

Doctors know that prompt diagnosis and treatment of Legionnaires' disease is key to a good outcome. More and more emergency rooms today have urine antigen test kits available. For a patient who has a positive urine antigen test, antibiotic treatment within 24 hours can improve outcome dramatically, as reported by researchers who studied the outcome of over 180 people infected with *Legionella* at a Dutch flower and home product show in 1999. (See case study).

Newer macrolides, such as azithromycin and clarithromycin, have replaced erythromycin as the standard treatment for adults with Legionnaires' disease since the mid-1990s. Certain fluoroquinolones have been shown to be effective in cases of severe disease that do not respond to macrolides. In patients who have not responded to **monotherapy** (use of one

(continued on page 62)

CASE STUDY:
Legionnaires' Disease at a Dutch Flower Show—A Study in Treatment Options

Westfriesian Flora, an annual flower and home products show in the Netherlands, is one of the premier shows of its kind in Europe. In February 1999, however, the show became the site of one of the largest outbreaks of community-acquired Legionnaires' disease in history. At least 188 people developed Legionnaires' disease, which was traced to a contaminated whirlpool bath in one home product exhibit.

The Netherlands has one of the best public health systems in Europe, and doctors and researchers used the opportunity presented by the 1999 flower show outbreak to conduct important research into the effectiveness of both testing and treatment for Legionnaires' disease. The results of this research have saved numerous lives as emergency room doctors have started to routinely use a quick urine test to diagnose Legionnaires' disease and to reduce the time between the onset of symptoms and the time when a patient begins to get appropriate treatment.

On March 9, 1999, Dutch health officials alerted the population through a special radio and television broadcast, and through newspapers, of an outbreak of Legionnaires' disease occurring at that time. The announcement noted that the flower show was the probable source of the outbreak. Authorities urged anyone suffering from fever, cough, chest pain, difficulty breathing, or other symptoms of Legionnaires' disease to go to the hospital for tests.

The Academic Medical Center in Amsterdam began a study of patients who had been diagnosed and those who would be diagnosed in the near future. Almost all those who had confirmed diagnoses of Legionnaires' disease (or, in cases where patients had died, their relatives) gave consent for the researchers to conduct interviews and to review medical records.

CASE STUDY: *(continued)*
Legionnaires' Disease at a Dutch Flower Show—A Study in Treatment Options

After the researchers excluded certain patients for a variety of reasons, they were left with 161 patients who had been diagnosed with Legionnaires' disease and treated as inpatients at a variety of hospitals. All of the patients had been visitors to the flower show; no employees of the exhibitors or exhibition center staff were diagnosed.

The study was designed to answer a number of questions concerning whether patients had better outcomes if they were treated in particular ways. They collected data on:

- Risk factors, such as cigarette smoking, and whether these had an effect on the necessity of intensive care unit (ICU) treatment

- "Pre-morbid" conditions, such as chronic lung disease or a suppressed immune system; and whether these had an effect on the necessity of ICU treatment

- Whether patients' symptoms at the time of hospital admission through the emergency room were "severe," defined as at least one of the following:

- Respiration rate less than 30 breaths per minute

  > Systolic blood pressure less than 90 mmHg or diastolic pressure less than 60 mmHg

  > Arterial oxygen saturation less than 92%

  > Chest X-ray that showed involvement of both lungs or involvement of more than one lobe of one lung

- Whether diagnosis was obtained using a *Legionella* antigen urine quick test or another, slower laboratory test

- The time between the hospital admission and the time of appropriate treatment with antibiotics (this is caused by the lag time in getting results from laboratory tests)

- Whether a negative urine antigen test, followed by a positive result on a different laboratory test and the resulting delay in treatment produced the same outcome as a lag before initial treatment for a person who did not receive a urine antigen test, but only conventional laboratory tests

The demographics of patients who became ill in this outbreak were typical of Legionnaires' disease outbreaks. Patients ranged in age from 21 to 92, with an average age of 67. Fifty-eight percent were men, and 62% had at least one underlying chronic illness. A history of cigarette smoking, a fever of over 102° Fahrenheit at the time of admission, and bilateral lung involvement were shown to be predictors of admission to the ICU and a higher rate of death. Although the chest X-rays of 40% of patients showed more extensive involvement 24 to 48 hours after admission than at the time of admission, this result was not associated with a higher rate of ICU admission or death. However, renal insufficiency (kidney failure), which occurred in 35% of patients after admission, was associated with a higher rate of ICU admission and death (Figure 6.1).

Among the other results the researchers found were:

- The mortality rate (percentage of patients who died) for the 141 patients in the study was 13%; for the 40 patients admitted to the ICU, the mortality rate was 36%

- There was no significant difference in the average incubation period for patients whose illness was characterized as "severe" and those who had less severe illness

CASE STUDY: *(continued)*
Legionnaires' Disease at a Dutch Flower Show—A Study in Treatment Options

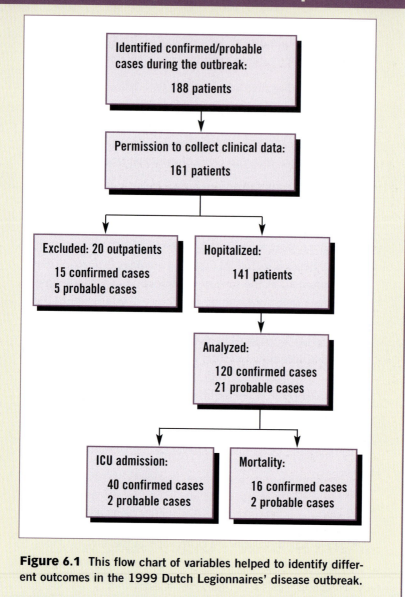

Figure 6.1 This flow chart of variables helped to identify different outcomes in the 1999 Dutch Legionnaires' disease outbreak.

- There was no significant difference in the average incubation period for patients who were admitted to the ICU and recovered and those who were admitted to the ICU and died

- The 71 patients who went to the hospital after the national alert were generally less ill than those who had gone to the hospital before the alert (21% of those who went after the alert had disease characterized as "severe" as opposed to 44% who went to the hospital before the alert)

The results of various therapies were the most important findings to come out of this study. Those who were treated with adequate antibiotic therapy within 24 hours after admission were less likely to need ICU care than those whose adequate antibiotic treatment did not begin until more than 24 hours after admission. This difference in ICU-free survival rate was not explained by differences in severity of pneumonia, risk factors, or pre-morbid conditions. The only difference was how quickly the antibiotic therapy was started.

The standard urinary antigen test can provide diagnosis within one hour, as opposed to the 4 days it takes to grow *Legionella* on culture from a sputum sample. Blood tests can provide antigen results in 12 to 24 hours, more quickly if laboratory work is expedited.

In this study, the urine antigen test was positive in 86 of the 141 patients, negative in 51 patients, and not performed in four patients. In 35 patients who had a negative urine antigen test, other tests produced positive results, whereas 16 patients showed no positive laboratory studies, despite clinical symptoms that strongly suggested Legionnaires' disease.

CASE STUDY: (continued)
Legionnaires' Disease at a Dutch Flower Show—A Study in Treatment Options

Patients with negative urine antigen tests, whether or not other tests were positive for *Legionella*, had a higher ICU-free survival rate than patients with positive urine antigen tests. There was no effect on the outcome of patients with negative urine antigen tests if antibiotic therapy was delayed until there was a positive result on another laboratory test. However, there was a definite effect of delaying antibiotic treatment more than 24 hours despite a positive urine antigen test— such patients had a much higher incidence of ICU treatment and of death.

These last results are the most important for current treatment of Legionnaires' disease. Doctors can infer from these results that, in fact, a positive urine antigen test is a greater indicator of the severity of the disease than are the clinical symptoms. They can also infer that in such severe cases, time is critical: starting antibiotic treatment immediately can be the difference between life and death.

(continued from page 56)

drug), doctors have used a combination of rifampin and erythromycin.

Most antibiotics are administered **intravenously** (through a vein) for the first few days of treatment. After the patient shows signs of responding to the treatment, he or she is switched to oral antibiotics for the duration of treatment, which is generally 2 weeks for cases that are not severe and 3 weeks for severe cases or for patients who are immuno-compromised. In some instances, there is a need for surgery to drain pockets of fluid in the lungs or in other areas where disease is present.

7

Prevention Is Key

Keeping water systems free of *L. pneumophila* is the key to reducing the number of people who contract Legionnaires' disease each year, but this is easier said than done. Some scientists predict that if every institutional potable water source and every evaporative cooling tower for an industrial air conditioner in the entire United States were sampled during the summer months, as many as 40% would test positive for *L. pneumophila*. Does this mean that such testing should be done, and that routine decontamination of all potential harbors of *Legionella* is necessary?

If it is true that 40% of samples would be positive, why don't more people become ill with Legionnaires' disease? The answer to this question is complex. Maybe more people do become ill, but their illness is not attributed to *Legionella*. Maybe most people who are exposed to *Legionella* simply do not become ill. Maybe *Legionella* is able to produce disease only when it is present in significant concentrations, or only when combined with certain atmospheric conditions.

Scientists at the federal Centers for Disease Control and Prevention (CDC) in Atlanta, and other experts on Legionnaires' disease, believe that Legionnaires' disease is, in fact, the cause of anywhere from 3% to 15% of all cases of community-acquired pneumonia in the United States. This amounts to somewhere between 8,000 and 18,000 cases per year by some estimates.

Only about 300 to 400 confirmed cases of Legionnaires' disease are diagnosed each year throughout the country, however. Part of this is because, despite the efforts of public health officials, primary care and emergency room doctors do not conduct detailed tests of most patients who walk into their office or their emergency room with pneumonia. They treat the pneumonia with an antibiotic and do not necessarily seek the cause. This is also true for hospital-acquired Legionnaires' disease, although more hospitals are becoming rigorous in their testing of patients who become ill with pneumonia

CASE STUDY: Legionnaires' Disease in a Maryland Hotel

On December 1, 2003, the Worcester County Health Department on the Eastern Shore of Maryland notified the Maryland Department of Health and Mental Hygiene and the federal Centers for Disease Control and Prevention in Atlanta of two confirmed cases of Legionnaires' disease in Maryland residents who had vacationed at one particular hotel. The two initial cases, in Ocean City, had stayed at the same hotel for 3 to 4 days each, within one day of each other.

Maryland has one of the most sophisticated tracking systems for cases of Legionnaires' disease. As part of this enhanced surveillance, doctors who treat patients suspected of having Legionnaires' disease interview the patients about their location, accommodations, and any travel they have taken in the 10 days prior to visiting the doctor.

Hotels have been a common location for outbreaks of Legionnaires' disease (the original outbreak from which the disease derived its name occurred in a Philadelphia hotel in 1976) and the CDC estimates that approximately 21% of Legionnaires' disease cases annually are associated with travel.

Local health authorities and later the CDC conducted an environmental survey of the hotel, and took multiple samples at four different times from various points in the hotel's water system. Many of these samples came back positive for *L. pneumophila* serotype 1 (Lp1), all with the same subtype as identified by monoclonal antibodies. Positive samples were found in the hotel's hot water storage tank, a number of hot

while hospitalized. Part of the reason for such a low official count of Legionnaires' cases annually is that individual confirmed cases are not always brought to the attention of the CDC, which keeps the official records.

water heaters, the air conditioning cooling tower, and at various other points including some faucets and showerheads.

By February 2004, seven confirmed cases and one possible case of Legionnaires' disease had been discovered in guests who had stayed at the hotel between October and early February. The seven people who became ill had rooms in different wings and on different floors of the hotel. One case occurred after the hotel conducted its first remediation attempt in January 2004.

The January remediation included superheating all hotel water systems, flushing all water taps, and hyperchlorinating the air conditioning cooling tower. Showers and sink faucets were disinfected with a bleach solution, and showerheads and sink aerators in the rooms where the patients had stayed were changed.

After the third and fourth cases were found, a second remediation occurred in February. Again, the hotel superheated and flushed the water systems. All showerheads and necks, as well as faucets, were disinfected again. The sand filter in the whirlpool spa was cleaned. In March, the hotel's potable water system was super-chlorinated, and a postremediation monitoring plan was instituted.

After the final remediation in March 2004, no further cases of Legionnaires' disease occurred at the hotel. In the summer of 2004, low levels of *L. pneumophila* were found in a sample from the air conditioning cooling tower, and another round of hyperchlorination was conducted.

Regardless of the reasons for the difference between the number of annual confirmed cases and the number of annual suspected cases, the big question really is whether or not Legionnaires' disease is preventable, and—if it is—whether it is preventable at a reasonable cost.

After the outbreak of Legionnaires' disease at a New York City university hospital, the discovery of *Legionella* in the potable water system of another New York City hospital (without any cases of illness) and another outbreak about 20 miles north of the city at a suburban community hospital, the New York State Department of Health issued new guidelines for hospitals. The health department ordered hospitals to sample both their potable water systems and any air conditioning cooling towers for *Legionella* twice a year (four times a year for hospitals with transplant services or for those where an outbreak had occurred in the past) and to decontaminate the water system if any samples tested positive.

The state of Maryland has long had even more rigorous guidelines for hospitals throughout the state, and in Allegheny County, Pennsylvania, in and around Pittsburgh, the guidelines are even stricter. Pittsburgh is the home of Dr. Victor Yu, Chief of Infectious Diseases at the Veterans Administration Medical Center, the country's foremost expert on Legionnaires' disease, and a consultant to hospitals and health officials around the country.

WHAT DOES DECONTAMINATION ENTAIL?

Emergency decontamination after the discovery of *Legionella* generally takes one of two forms, superheating and hyperchlorination.

Superheating

Environmental surveys for *Legionella* in hospital water supplies have found it present in between 12% and 70% of samples. The bottom of hot water tanks is an especially popular place for the bacteria to grow, with the usual **biofilm** (a nutrient-rich layer of slime that sinks to the bottom of water tanks), sediments, and other microorganisms that grow in such an environment. Higher concentrations of calcium and magnesium were associated with greater concentrations of *L. pneumophila* in a study of 15 hospitals.

Studies that have modeled *L. pneumophila* in plumbing systems have found it able to live very well at 20°, 30°, 40°, and 50° Celsius; at 60° Celsius there is no evidence of *Legionella*. Studies of *Legionella* colonization of home plumbing and heating have shown that the tendency of *L. pneumophila* to colonize the bottom of water heaters heated by electricity more often than those heated by natural gas or oil,

CASE STUDY: Legionnaires' Disease at a Michigan Prison

During August and September 1993, 17 people at a state prison in Michigan—16 inmates and one employee—were diagnosed with Legionnaires' disease. All were infected with *Legionella pneumophila* serotype 1 (Lp1), with the same subtype as defined by monoclonal antibody subtyping.

Samples were taken of the prison's potable water supply, as well as from the cooling tower on top of the prison hospital, and from a community cooling tower near the prison. Only the cooling tower on top of the prison hospital tested positive for *Legionella*; the isolates from the sample matched those from laboratory samples taken from the sick inmates and employee.

Fourteen of the inmates with Legionnaires' disease had used the outdoor exercise areas within 100 yards of the prison hospital (a total of 2,253 inmates used those exercise areas), whereas only two inmates (of 2,270) who used the exercise areas on the other side of the prison, at least 400 yards from the cooling tower, were infected with *Legionella*.

The cooling tower was shut down and decontaminated, and no further cases were reported.

because of the placement of the heating coils several inches above the bottom of the tank.

Institutional potable water systems can be superheated and flushed to kill *Legionella*. Hot water storage tanks and water heaters that are not running hot enough have been shown to harbor colonies of *Legionella*, as have the distal ends (faucets and showerheads) of potable water systems. Super-heating to kill a *Legionella* bloom entails getting the water to 70° Celsius (158° Fahrenheit), opening all of the faucets and showerheads (where the temperature must reach 60° Celsius), and flushing the system for 30 minutes. After an episode of superheating and flushing, unless the hot water is maintained at 60° Celsius consistently, *L. pneumophila* often recurs within months.

Hyperchlorination

The other method of emergency decontamination used in potable water systems, and in emergency decontamination of water towers and cooling towers, is "shock" hyperchloriniza-tion. In this method, a large amount of chlorine is put into a water system that is already chlorinated to generate a con-centration of 20 to 50 parts per million (ppm) of chlorine, followed by draining the system and refilling it.

Continuous Decontamination

Other methods are used for continuous decontamination of water systems.

Continuous hyperchlorination involves raising the con-tinuous chlorine level in the potable water system to more than 3 ppm, which has been shown to suppress the growth of *L. pneumophila* (unlike the standard chlorine level of 1 ppm).

Chlorine does not kill *L. pneumophila*, it merely suppresses it. Recolonization often occurs after a shock hyperchlorination. In continuous chlorination, recolonization can occur rapidly if the chlorinator malfunctions.

Copper/silver ionization is a **bactericidal** method that uses positively charged ions of these heavy metals to bind with negatively charged sites on cell walls, which creates stress on the cells and a chain reaction that leads to cell death. A small computer maintains the continuous pulse of charged copper/silver ions into the water supply. Hundreds of institutions have installed the $60,000 to $100,000 units. The heavy metal ions used in this method have no negative impact on human health, although it is possible that long-term use could create *Legionella* bacteria that become resistant to these ions.

Ultraviolet light generated at 254 nanometers has been shown to kill bacteria by hampering DNA replication. Ultraviolet irradiation units are installed at the distal points of use in a water system; the water passes through the ultraviolet light unit before proceeding to the faucets and showerheads. Ultraviolet light works best as an adjunct to other systemic decontamination methods such as superheating and flushing. The units do not affect water quality or plumbing.

Instantaneous heating systems, sometimes called "flash" heating systems, kill *L. pneumophila* by heating water to a temperature of around 190° Fahrenheit (88° Celsius) then blending the superheated water with cold water to produce water of the desired temperature.

Flash heating has had mixed results. In a study of 15 hospitals, the two that used flash heating were *Legionella*-free, whereas nine of the other 13 hospitals had positive samples in water tanks and at distal faucets. However a hospital that had previously had an outbreak of Legionnaires' disease and changed from conventional hot water delivery to flash heating still showed evidence of *Legionella* at distal sites.

Experts recommend that hospitals use more than one method simultaneously. Such **redundancy** provides the best possibility of reducing the chances of future Legionnaires' disease outbreaks.

Glossary

Aerosolized—Distributed as droplets or particles through the air.

Aspirate—To inhale fluid into the lungs.

Aspiration—The entry of secretions or foreign material into the trachea and lungs.

Assay—A laboratory test for determining the properties or actions of a material.

Bactericidal—Having the ability to kill bacteria.

Biofilm—A layer of microorganisms that has grown on a surface.

Cilia—Tiny, hairlike projections that line the surface of many organs, including those of the respiratory system.

Direct fluorescent antibody (DFA) test—A laboratory test used to identify pathogens in clinical samples, in which antibodies are combined with a fluorescent dye that glows when the target organism is present.

Endemic—Native to or occurring in a particular area.

Endocarditis—Inflammation of the lining of the heart.

Epidemiology—The study of the occurrence, causes, frequency, and distribution of diseases in human populations.

Extrapulmonary—Occurring outside the lungs.

Facultative—Able to live or function under different environmental conditions.

Gram stain—A laboratory test used to identify certain types of bacteria.

Hyponatremia—An abnormally low level of sodium the blood.

Immunocompromised—The state of having decreased or deactivated immune function.

Immunosuppression—A decrease or deactivation of the immune system.

Immunosuppressive drug—A medication that decreases or deactivates the action of the body's immune system.

Intravenous—Medication given through a needle placed directly into a vein.

Intubation—The process of placing a breathing tube into a patient.

Macrolides—A category of antibiotic drugs.

Macrophage—A type of white blood cell that makes up part of the immune system and is responsible for destroying microorganisms that invade the body.

Monoclonal antibody—Man-made antibody that is designed to interact with one specific protein, often used to identify pathogens from clinical samples.

Monotherapy—Treatment with a single drug or therapy.

Mortality rate—The proportion of deaths associated with a disease.

Mucociliary action—Process by which bacteria are cleared from the respiratory system through the movement of tiny hairlike projections that line the respiratory organs.

Myocarditis—Inflammation of the heart muscle.

Myocardium—The muscles of the heart.

Palliative care—Treatment given to patients with life-threatening, chronic illness, which focuses on pain relief and patient comfort rather than cure.

Pathogen—A microorganism that can cause disease.

Pericarditis—Inflammation of the tissues surrounding the heart.

Polymerase chain reaction (PCR)—A laboratory test used to detect small amounts of genetic material in a clinical sample.

Potable—Safe to drink.

Prospective study—Study design where one or more groups who do not have a disease or condition are monitored to assess the number of instances of the disease or condition occur over time.

Quinolones—A category of antibiotic drugs used to treat bacteria that are resistant to traditionally used antibiotics.

Redundancy—The design of a system in such a way that it can continue to function even when components fail or break.

Renal insufficiency—Failure of the kidneys to function properly in excreting wastes from the body.

Retrospective study—A study based on the medical records of patients who have the disease or conditioned being examined.

Rifampin—An antibiotic drug.

Serotype—Any of a group of closely related microorganisms that share common chemical characteristics.

Sputum—Mucus that is coughed up from the lungs.

Superinfection—The presence of more than one infectious disease.

Symptomatically—Treating as the symptom of a disease.

Tetracyclines—A category of antibiotic drugs.

Titer—The amount or concentration of a particular substance or material.

Bibliography

Marre, R., et. al., editors. *Legionella*. American Society of Microbiology, 2001.

Health and Safety Executives, *Prevention or Control of* Legionellosis, *Including Legionnaires' Disease*. Health and Safety Executives, 2001.

Further Reading

Stout J. and Yu, V. L. "*Legionellosis*: Current Concepts." *New England Journal of Medicine.* September 4, 1997.

Sabria M. and Yu, V. L. "Hospital-Acquired *Legionellosis*: Solutions for a Preventable Infection." *The Lancet Infectious Diseases.* June 2002.

"Legionnaires' Disease Outbreak in Murcia, Spain." *Emerging Infectious Diseases.* Atlanta, GA: U.S. Department of Health and Human Services, CDC. August 2003.

"Legionnaires' Disease at a Dutch Flower Show." *Emerging Infectious Diseases.* December 2002.

"Legionnaires' Disease Appears at a Hospital in New Rochelle." *The New York Times,* July 15, 2005.

"Hospitals are Asked to Decontaminate Water." *The New York Times,* July 20, 2005.

Websites

http://www.cdc.gov
Centers for Disease Control and Prevention

http://www.ncbi.nlm.nih.gov
National Library of Medicine, National Institutes of Health

http://www.e-medicine.com

http://medic.med.uth.tmc.edu
University of Texas Health System

http://genome4.cpmc.columbia.edu
Columbia Genome Center, Columbia University

http://www.legionella.org

Index

Page numbers in *italic* type indicate illustrations.

Index

Index

superheating decontami-
nation method, 66–68
supermarket outbreak,
30–33
surgical treatment, 62
surgical wound infections,
49
symptoms, 25, 47, 49, 54,
58

tests, diagnostic. *See*
diagnostic tests
tetracycline antibiotics,
56
tobacco use, as risk factor,
23, 39, 59
transplant patients, 13,
38, 47, 49
treatment, 54, 56, 61, 62

treatment outcomes
study, 57–62

ultraviolet light decontamination, 69
urinary antigen test, 26,
41, 56, 58, 59, 61–62

Veterans Administration
(VA) hospitals out-
break, 13
viral pneumonia, 9
Virginia home improve-
ment store outbreak,
49–52

water, *Legionella* species
in, 23. *See also* potable
water

water heaters, 67
water systems
decontamination of,
28–29, 65, 66–69
as *Legionella* source,
14, 23, 35, 37–38,
63, 64–65
water towers, decontami-
nation of, 68
whirlpool baths, 48,
51–52, 57–62
wound infections, 49

X-ray, pneumonia, 9

Yu, Victor, 34, 36, 37, 40,
66

zones of exposure, 44

About the Authors

Laurel Shader, M.D., is chair of pediatrics at the Fair Haven Community Health Center in New Haven, Connecticut and Clinical Assistant Professor at the Yale University School of Medicine and Yale University School of Nursing.

Jon Zonderman, her husband, is an independent writer/editor who specializes in health care, science/technology, and business.

About the Founding Editor

The late **I. Edward Alcamo** was a Distinguished Teaching Professor of Microbiology at the State University of New York at Farmingdale. Alcamo studied biology at Iona College in New York and earned his M.S. and Ph.D. degrees in microbiology at St. John's University, also in New York. He had taught at Farmingdale for over 30 years. In 2000, Alcamo won the Carski Award for Distinguished Teaching in Microbiology, the highest honor for microbiology teachers in the United States. He was a member of the American Society for Microbiology, the National Association of Biology Teachers, and the American Medical Writers Association. Alcamo authored numerous books on the subjects of microbiology, AIDS, and DNA technology as well as the award-winning textbook *Fundamentals of Microbiology*, now in its sixth edition.